For Jane,

Words could never describe
the thanks which I owe to you.

With love always.

Adam x

Doves, Pigeons
&
Masonry Bees

An historical encounter with
St. Mary Magdalene Church, Trimdon Village

ADAM LUKE

With written contributions from historian John Grundy
and former Prime Minister Tony Blair.

First published 2011

The author would like to thank all of the people who have
contributed, without whom this publication would not have been
possible.

The author wishes to thank Mr. Grundy and Mr. Blair for their
written contributions to his publication.

Part-funded by Cllr. Peter Brookes, Members Initiative Fund.

© Cover design by David Spears from an original photograph by
Malcolm Schofield.

© Illustrations by G. Defty.

Edited by R. M. Batty.

ISBN 978-1-907257-21-6

Printed in 2011 by
Quoin Publishing Ltd.,
17 North Street, Middlesbrough
TS2 1JP

For all those people who love
St. Mary Magdalene, find pleasure within
her walls and hold her at the centre of their hearts.

Table of Contents

Foreword

By John Grundy

I first came across Adam Luke when he turned up at a meeting of The Friends of Beamish Museum. He was a young teenager at the time and to get to the meeting he had needed to cross half of County Durham by bus on a particularly cold and unpleasant day – a feat I wouldn't have liked to attempt myself. You can imagine that I was impressed by such dedication to history, local culture and the built environment.

The second time I met him was because he had invited me to draw the prizes in a Grand Summer Draw which he had organised to raise funds towards the provision of an accessible toilet at St. Mary Magdalene. I have to tell you that this was a terrific experience. Adam had winkled impressive prizes out of a whole host of local people and institutions; on top of that he'd got me there and also persuaded Bert Draycott, the world spoon playing champion, to be on hand to entertain the troops, but what made the event really special was the sense of community that prevailed in the church. The place was packed, the mood happy and animated, the amount of money raised seriously impressive. If you go to the church now you'll see the outcome of that event and all the others like it, many of which involved Adam as well. The loo and the extended vestry are in use, the church fully fitted as a 21st century building, utterly suitable still as a place of worship but equipped to fulfil all of the other duties that are expected of a parish church in the modern world.

I have to admit that until that visit I had never been to Trimdon Church. I had driven past it and been impressed by its pretty setting on an island site in the middle of the village's attractive green but I had never been inside. I have now, and I'm delighted to say that it is a lovely church – Norman in its fabric with bits and pieces from many centuries since. It was enriched in Victorian times and early in the 20th century and, of course, it is still changing today, 850 years after the first stones were laid.

I hope you enjoy this book. I hope you recognise the love and the passion with which it was written and, above all, I hope you enjoy your time in the village of Trimdon and the beautiful church at its heart.

John Grundy

Introduction

It is with great pleasure that I bring you this insight into the amazing and much anticipated history of the church and village we know and love today. All those many hundreds of years ago when settlers chose this, the highest point on the coastal plain at 569 feet, to build the village that would become Trimdon, they knew little of the turbulent and wonderfully diverse future ahead. Some years later, a church was built, probably in wood, and Trimdon's connection with Christianity began. In 1145 local people used local materials and provided a building which has grown to form a part of my heart: a sentiment echoed through many villagers! It is a church in which I do not only feel a sense of reassurance, safety and compassion, but contentment at not only the architecture but the power of community spirit combined with Christian tradition. From the laying of the very first stone so many things have changed: socially, emotionally and physically. The church has been a window to the transition from minute Roman settlement to a modern village recovering from the effect of employment change. It has also so importantly protected the religious believers of this parish and been their friend through times of need and times of joy. It is one of only a few buildings which I could personally describe as outstanding in every sense, which, when combined with the warm and friendly welcome, provides a wonderful place of worship. With that firmly in mind, I would like to take this opportunity to thank you for joining me on this journey through a remarkable history.

Yours

Adam Luke

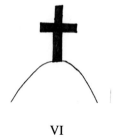

VI

Chapter I

Is it Tremeduna?

In order to peer into the incredible history of St. Mary Magdalene Church, we must first look to the history of Trimdon and of the local area. Trimdon Village or Old Trimdon is the oldest of the Trimdons with its roots in farming and agriculture. The additions of Trimdon Grange and Trimdon Colliery come much later around the mining industry. Throughout this book we will mainly focus on Old Trimdon. Trimdon Village is a small former mining community with approximately 1,400 houses, located four miles north-east of Sedgefield and approximately 250 miles north of London. The village is of considerable age even though it was first recorded by Bishop Pudsey in 1147.

The presence of civilised humans in the North East can date to approximately 500BC. At this time and until the Roman Invasion, Britain was a land of tribes; the North East was inhabited by a tribe named the Brigantes who were led by Cartimandua.

In the 1950s, during the building of the local authority estate, Roman artefacts were discovered on the site of Tremeduna Grange which became sheltered accommodation, implying the site has been occupied for much longer. The Romans had ruled the ancient kingdom of Northumbria for three-and-a-half centuries, ending in the 300s AD. The 43AD invasion brought with it the great Roman culture, but more important to this book is that they brought Christianity. Constantine was the first emperor to introduce this new religion to Britain, removing the old Celtic traditions. By 314 York was one of the main Christian places in the Roman Empire. Within the next 300 years some Ancient Britons, Celts and others continued to practise their religions creating a Romano-British Culture by the end of Roman rule.

The name of Trimdon is recorded to have only been in use since the 17th century. Historic names before this included Tremledona in 1196 and Trembledon in 1339. "Treml" is thought to mean wooden cross and "don" the Anglo Saxon word for hill. Years of research by various historians have resulted in the theory that a wooden cross was erected by early Christians on the site of the later Anglo Saxon church. There is, however, much debate and another theory concludes that the "don" part of the name refers to the mound on which the church of St. Mary Magdalene is built. This theory also suggests that this mound could be the result of a pagan burial site[1].

During his reign, King Canute made a pilgrimage to the shrine of St. Cuthbert in Durham Cathedral. The history says that he began his bare-footed pilgrimage from Garmondsway Moor (North West of Trimdon) to Durham. Local legend states that King Canute visited Trimdon and rested here in order for him to trim his beard and don his cloak. The story goes that Trimdon became known as "The Place of Tonsure" and got its name from this[2]. Unfortunately, there is no evidence to support this exciting theory. King Canute also known as King Knut was born in 994. As well as being King of England he was King Canute 2nd of Denmark and King of Norway. As a result of his large contribution to the Viking Empire he is often referred to as Canute the Great. King Swein, Canute's father, invaded England in 1013 and upon his death the following year his eldest son Harold became King of the Empire. King Ethelred, the defeated King of England, was reinstated as monarch by the English people. 1015 saw the gathering of forces by Canute and a return to England to reclaim the throne; it was a success and he regained much of England but not London. The English council declared Canute King, however, London chose Edmund, Ethelred's son, as King of the district. Canute battled with Edmund until his death in

2

1016 and Canute gained control of the whole country. The next year in 1017 the King married Ethelred's widow to ensure that his sons did not regain the throne. To be certain that he would not lose the throne he engineered the death of his eldest son and pursued the others until they fled abroad. Upon the death of his brother in Denmark in 1019 he reclaimed his throne there. Sadly, seven years later, Canute was defeated at the battle of the Holy River in Denmark. Ulf, the then Danish King, was killed and Canute chased the Norwegian King, Olaf Haraldson 2nd and took the Norwegian crown. In November 1035 Canute died aged 40, his Empire disintegrated and the original royalty regained control.

There are many geographical reasons why Trimdon may have been chosen as the perfect site for a settlement. The first and most obvious being that it is situated on a hill, the benefit being that settlers could watch for invaders. Local legend states that the Watch Bank that separates Trimdon and Trimdon Grange got its name from this ability[3]; another is that the village lies 569 feet above sea level – the highest point on the Durham Coastal Plain and indeed the whole of Sedgefield Borough. The site can therefore be perceived to be of strategic importance to armies of invaders from the North Sea. In addition to its height, it is only ten miles from the North Sea. The final and most supported reason is that Trimdon is close to the source of the River Skerne. It is a tributary of the River Tees and is approximately 25 miles in length. After flowing through the valley between Trimdon and Trimdon Grange it joins Hurworth Burn and travels south to meet the River Tees at Hurworth Place in Hurworth on Tees. The source rises at Garmondsway Moor: just North West of the Village, nestled in the magnesium limestone hills. It is an unusual river due to the fact that it flows inland to join the Tees at Croft.

The population of Trimdon in 1801 was only 208, as the only Trimdon at the time was Old Trimdon (Trimdon Village) – a farming village. In the 1851 census the population stood at 382, but by the time of the 1861 census this had risen to 1,598. The sinking of Trimdon Grange Colliery and the formation of the new Trimdon Grange was the reason for this exponential growth. The population continued to grow and in 1891 the total was 4,135 people. Sadly, after the colliery closed in 1969, the population began to decline as people moved away for work. By the 1990s the Trimdon population increased to 5,000, as new transportation and road connections were formed to all North East towns and cities.

The population of the four Trimdons is now estimated at 5,000 people; however, population change has occurred throughout the last two centuries. Like the rest of the United Kingdom's population it is ageing in nature – the reason for this being the fall in crude death rate per thousand to just 10 in 2008. People are beginning to favour a career over starting a family and as a result the number of babies being born has decreased. Improved healthcare, cleaner and more hygienic living conditions have also contributed to longer life expectancy. This national pattern can be assumed to be mirrored in Trimdon with falling school enrolment numbers and a decreased number of funerals.

The North East's mining communities like Trimdon are known for their many traditional pastimes, for example pigeon racing. Some sources claim that this particular sport has its origins as long ago as 220AD. The sport is still enjoyed today by the people of the North East, although, as in all traditions, it is declining in membership. In 1881 the Royal Family took to the sport and has continued to take part ever since.

The new villages were blighted by poor living conditions. "The Plantation" was a housing estate in Trimdon Grange to house the miners and their families. The houses were unhygienic and crowded: sometimes up to 15 people in each house. The roads were unmade and mud often flooded the low-lying yards. The houses were overshadowed by the towering piles of waste rock from the sorting process at the mine. After a damning newspaper report in the early 1960s, in which local councillor George Terrans deemed the area: "Durham's little Hiroshima", the last of the houses were demolished. The pre-war Beveridge report by economist William Beveridge identified housing as an area of concern[4]. Clement Atlee's post-war Labour government established social housing as part of the new welfare state. Sedgefield Rural District Council began the construction of large estates of council houses. In Trimdon Village over 1,000 homes were constructed and many of those from "The Plantation" moved into these. This development continued in the 1970s with an extension to the estate completed along with three blocks of flats. Tremeduna Grange sheltered accommodation block was built on the site of a village farm and it was during its building that Roman artefacts were discovered. Other developments included the opening of Trimdon Secondary Modern (now Junior School) in 1958. This along with the new infant school which opened in 1957, replaced the Parochial School. Developments have continued to this day – with a new housing estate in 1998 and library and Cooperative store in 2004. Trimdon Village is an area striving to continue as a desirable place to live with a community second to none.

Chapter II

The Land of the Prince Bishops

After venturing into the history of Trimdon we must now place it into the larger context of County Durham – The Land of the Prince Bishops – and its diverse history. Variation and historical merit are woven into the fabric of County Durham life. It is the only English county to bear the word "County" in its title. The county, which is adored the world over, is aptly described in the book Heritage and History of Durham: *"County Durham has an inherent sense of identity and continuity which has evolved over many centuries. Shaped by a blend of Christian, Social and Industrial heritage, its unique character imparts a strong feeling of stability and belonging in a time of rapid change."* Durham County has witnessed an immense change of industry in the last 200 years, which has altered the county forever.

In Anglo Saxon times Great Britain was many different kingdoms and Durham belonged to one of the largest – Northumbria. It was famous for having great centres of art and early Christianity, producing famous saints such as Cuthbert and The Venerable Bede. Do not be misled by Northumbria being the modern Northumberland; the Anglo Saxon Northumbria was roughly what we now call North East England.

The County's geographical position in the North East is very simple; it is sandwiched between the densely populated Tyneside to the north and Teesside to the south. One of England's most northerly counties, Durham was once self-governed by the Prince Bishops. The Prince Bishops, or Kings of Durham as they are often referred to, virtually operated the county as a separate territory. A Prince

Bishop is a prince of the church – one of the highest ranked clergymen and higher even than an archbishop. The Durham Bishops inherited their powers from the earlier Bishops of Lindsfarne.

After a struggle to conquer the Earldom of Northumbria, William the Conqueror needed to protect this new conquest against invasion from Scotland. He began to protect it by removing the Saxon Earl and replacing him with one of his supporters: Robert de Commines. On his first day he was killed along with 700 of his supporters in Durham. After this event William replaced Robert with another Norman: Walter of Lorraine, who was also murdered. Walter met his end after being locked in a burning church in Gateshead. This infuriated William, resulting in him personally leading an army to Northumbria which resulted in the "Harrying of the North". After these events the new Bishop was called William de St. Carileph who later began the construction of Durham Cathedral.

The County Palatine of Durham was virtually a separate state and the Prince Bishop had nearly the same powers as the King of England. Holding his own parliament, raising his own army, levying his own taxes and minting his own coinage are only a few. The Prince Bishops' official residences were Durham Castle and Auckland Castle.

St. Mary Magdalene Church is now under the control of Durham Diocese, which was formed in 995AD. Bishop Aldrun was the first Bishop of the new diocese, consisting of approximately 250 parishes serving 1.5 million people throughout the North East in 300 churches. Durham Cathedral is, of course, the largest of these churches and part of the world-famous Durham World Heritage Site. The diocese is divided into three Archdeaconries, which are each in turn divided into deaneries and those into localities or parishes.

Durham County Council began its life under the Local Government Act of 1888. It brought together the boroughs of Durham, Stockton-on-Tees, Jarrow and West Hartlepool. West Hartlepool became a municipal county in 1902 followed by Darlington in 1915. Then in 1967 the county border with North Yorkshire was altered. It continued to lose territory with Gateshead transferring to Tyne and Wear and Billingham to Teesside. In 1972 the Local Government Act abolished the original boundaries. The new County Durham gained land from North Yorkshire and as a result the coat of arms gained a white rose (The Yorkshire Emblem), which still can be seen today in the centre of the County Council Logo. Durham was divided into smaller districts in a two-tier council system: Easington District, Sedgefield Borough, Durham City, Derwentside District, Teesdale District and Chester-le-Street District. This system was abolished in 2009 even though a 2007 referendum concluded that 76 per cent of the county wished to retain the old system. A new unitary authority was established dealing with all services.

The ancient kingdom of Northumbria and the Diocese of Durham have been a major influence on the great northern saints: The Venerable Bede, Hild, Oswald, Chad, Aidan and of course Cuthbert. St Cuthbert who is the patron saint of Durham City and the Diocese of Newcastle was born in 635. As a young boy Cuthbert tended sheep around the monastery where he lived. His real religious career was said to begin in 651 when he was tending his sheep and was subject to a vision of the soul of St. Aidan being carried to heaven by two angels. This career was put on hold as the ongoing threat of invasion to the vulnerable kingdom of Northumbria by the King of Mercia continued. As an able-bodied man he was called up to fight until peace was finally restored at the battle of Winwidfield. Finally, in 664, he was sent by St. Eata to be the prior at Lindsfarne in order to introduce the roman customs within the monastery. Whilst there, he evanglised the people and was said not to be able to conduct a mass without crying. In 676 he retired from his role and moved to

Farne Island where he lived in peace until he was sent for by a group of Bishops in 684. They brought him the news of his election as Bishop of Lindsfarne. Sadly, he resigned from his position in 686. He died in March 687. St. Cuthbert was buried in the monastery of Lindsfarne. 200 years later, when the Vikings invaded Northumbria, the monks fled with Cuthbert's remains. For eight years Cuthbert's coffin travelled with the fleeing Northumbrians until it was again laid to rest in Chester-le-Street. At the completion of Durham Cathedral the body was finally laid to rest. His shrine is visited at Durham Cathedral by millions of visitors and pilgrims alike.

Also lying in Durham Cathedral are the remains of the Venerable Bede, another famous saint of the North of England. Bede began his religious career as a monk at Wearmouth in Sunderland. The *Ecclesiastical History of the English People* was his most famous publication, earning him the title "The Father of English History". He died in a monastery in Jarrow in 735 and is celebrated on his feast day of 25 May.

The Christian religion continues in County Durham today. The county houses one of the greatest examples of early English Christian architecture in the form of 7th century wonder, Escomb Church. It is also home to pioneers of the latest in Christian mission: The Bethany Centre and Emmanuel Church are examples. The other 300 churches in the diocese cover everything in between. Escomb Church is believed to have been built in the 7th century. It is by far the oldest church in Northumbria and some even believe it to be the best preserved church of its kind in the whole of Northern Europe.

At the other end of the scale Durham houses pioneering centres of Christianity: The Bethany Christian Centre in Houghton-le-Spring is a *"meeting place for people who love and desire the living God, and for those who are seeking to find out the Christian Faith"*.[5] Although the church has been established for 100 years, its way of mission is contemporary and up to date. The Emmanuel Church's vision is *"To be a growing, charismatic, family church, with a world vision. As a family church, we are open to all and provide a warm welcome into a family atmosphere of fun. We seek to build the church by being open to the gifts that he has given us, and express our joy in many ways."*[6] The church attempts to involve the whole family and engages them in the love of God – fusing a future generation of dedicated Christians. These centres as examples provide an insight into the changing community and developing generations of the future of County Durham.

Durham Cathedral is considered the greatest Norman building in Britain and some even believe in Europe. The cathedral was built to house the remains of and ultimately become a shrine to St. Cuthbert. The very first block was laid in 1093, the majority of the nave was completed in 1104 and the Galilee Chapel in 1133. With the main fabric of the building completed it wasn't until the early 13th century that the western towers were added. The largest tower was added in 1487. The cathedral has had a long and turbulent history including: being closed in the civil war by Oliver Cromwell and almost being bombed in World War 2. The latter was considered a miracle by the locals as on the night the bombing was planned, a thick fog covered the City of Durham. The cathedral joins St. Mary Magdalene and many other local treasures to enhance the historical landscape of Durham County – The Land of the Prince Bishops.

The annual sponsored knit in aid of The Children's Society.

Rededication of the memorial to those killed in the Trimdon Grange Explosion, in the presence of the Bishop in 1991.

The Christingle service is a popular Christmas event.

Mrs. McDonough retires after many, many years of service as organist in 1993.

Chapter III

Magnesium Limestone and The Normans

Before we can look at St. Mary Magdalene we must look at the geology of the local area, which provided its building stones.

The geology of County Durham and Northumberland is somewhat intriguing and is of scientific importance. The area of rock formed approximately 290-350 million years ago is of the type named carboniferous. The term comes from the rocks which are naturally high in carbon as they fall in areas with high levels of coal. After the ice age, the ice melted and formed a sea which stretched from the North East to Poland, according to some sources. This sea is known by scientists as the Zechstein Sea. When the temperature began to rise the water evaporated and left the complex layers of what is known as magnesium limestone: a buff-coloured stone found in the Trimdon area. There were other rocks formed during this period such as hard sandstones and soft mudstones, some of which can be seen in the fabric of St. Mary Magdalene. The most famous and scientifically important of these being the unique magnesium limestone which has an unusual chemical makeup; it is a limestone that is high in magnesium carbonate – different to other limestones. In Trimdon Grange Quarry this rock would be present but also ooidal limestone and subordinate dolomite. During the formation process a thick triangular belt of magnesium limestone 8km in width was formed in the Trimdon area. The unique geology led the area to be protected in 1992 as a site of special scientific interest. The unusual soil types have led to rare and unique plants including quaking grass *Briza Media*, blue moor grass *Sesleria Albicans* and wild carrot *Daucas Carota*. Furthermore, it is also part of the 270 hectares of magnesium limestone grassland remaining in the UK. The magnesium limestone cliffs that make up the County Durham coastline are the only examples in the United Kingdom and indeed the whole of Europe.

The area is still used for quarrying today in Coxhoe on Garmondsway Moor, owned by Tarmac UK Ltd., with main outputs of dolomite and limestone. However, there were other industrial quarries in the area which are now reclaimed as nature reserves. Trimdon Grange Quarry is located in the Magnesium Limestone Natural Area and is therefore protected. Experts believe that only 200 hectares remain today.

St. Mary Magdalene is constructed of a huge variety of different types of local stone with the main being carboniferous sandstone. This has commonly been used throughout history as a building tool as it is a durable material but can also be easily carved. Magnesium limestone is another stone used in the church. It can be clearly seen in the south eastern corner of the church. The walls are of considerable thickness, in some places up to 0.9 metres wide.

The church seems to have been built in the 12th century. When the 12th century began Trimdon would have been merely a very small hamlet on a great hill near the sea but by the end of this century the village had a humble little church which would transform over the years into the masterpiece we see today. The 12th century structure is barely recognisable today but in fact a lot of the stonework is still original. The majority of the original fabric is in the chancel and the south wall of the nave. The most obvious features that survive from that first Norman church are the chancel arch and the small round-headed window on the south side of the chancel.

In the word "Tremeldon", from which Trimdon is derived, the "Tremel" refers to a wooden cross. The wooden cross is thought to have been erected by early Christians. If this is correct, it shows that the site of St. Mary Magdalene was of religious significance even before the construction of the church.

During the last century historians believed that the "don" referred to a pagan mound or even a burial ground – this can be assumed to mean the mound that the church is situated on. This is now thought to be unlikely and nobody really knows how the mound came to be there. What is plainly clear is the Normans transformed English Churches and have left their mark on Trimdon.

Chapter IV

Lepers, Hugh de Puiset and Stained Glass

It is clear that St. Mary Magdalene was established in a period of uncertainty yet a period of history that can be considered to have established the very institutions and ways of life that still grace the country today. The Middle Ages is the time which starts from the fall of the Roman Empire. It is commonly referred to as the time between the 5th and 15th centuries. In brief, it was a time of rediscovery of many scriptures and artefacts lost during the Dark Ages.

It is a period of time that is highly relevant to this book as it was the time when Christianity became important within Europe. It was not, however, a safe time with invasions to the kingdom of Northumbria by the Vikings from Norway. In addition to it being important for the religion as a whole it was also during this time that St. Mary Magdalene was built. Trimdon can be considered to follow the pattern of other settlements after the 11th century with the new invention of Feudalism making agriculture more powerful.

After this brief period of rest, Britain was invaded from the south by the Normans at the Battle of Hastings in 1066. William the Conqueror, as he became known, settled in the south of the country. In time he progressed north, removing the tribes. The influence of the invasion was enormous with sources stating that not one house was left standing between York and Durham. The Prince Bishops on the other hand continued to be a huge force, with the famous Bishop Hugh Pudsey continuing to expand the number of possessions. The period was important for the region as mining had its origins – not in coal, which came later, but in silver and lead which were mined in Weardale. At the end of the period the county was left without the Prince Bishops and was reliant on the palace of Henry VIII.

With the building of the church occurring in the early centuries of this period to the standard of which has already been described, the church was updated to meet new styles and new fashions. According to the sketch plan completed by Durham Diocesan Architect C. Downes, the church was heavily altered. On the western wall, the most notable change was the construction of the bell cote. The church had no windows with the exception of one small round-headed one on the southern side of the chancel.

A common feature throughout Norman and early English-styled churches is a low-level, round-headed window and over the years this little window in St. Mary Magdalene Church has become the subject of much debate. There are two major theories about its original purpose, the first being that it was an opening through which a hand bell was rung to notify the start of the Elevation of the Host. The second more common theory is that it was the opening through which lepers would receive Holy Communion. The idea being that it is sited in that position to allow the leper to see the altar and to take part in the service without infecting others[7].

Leprosy is one of the oldest recorded diseases, attacking the nervous system. Today there are estimated to be 830,000 cases worldwide but the disease was prevalent in the Middle Ages with no known cause and no cure could be found. The only treatment was with isolation from families and communities. The church, by this point, was a very rich organisation and funded hospitals for the disease, with treatments including prayer and spiritual healings. Sherburn House near Durham is an example of one of these. The Black Death killed many of the lepers off and by the 16th century lepers were almost unheard of.

The question arising from the leper theory is: *how many lepers would there be in a small village like Trimdon?* Therefore the little window could have been installed as a precautionary measure. The other problem is, if it was a hagioscope (an opening in order to see the Elevation of the Host from outside), it would have been set at an angle: in St. Mary Magdalene it is not.

Some sources claim that prior to the 1873 alterations, this window was covered by a metal shutter[8]. Whatever its past, it is now a beautiful stained glass window dedicated as a gift from Edward Hardy (Churchwarden, 1873) and depicting St. Mary Magdalene.

Aerial shot of the site where Roman artefacts were found, now Tremeduna Grange Sheltered Accommodation.

Left: Organist Mrs McDonough plays the new organ for the first time in 1982. Below: Tommy Hudson keeps the churchyard tidy.

Right: Prime Minster Tony Blair pictured with Mrs M. Robinson MBE, who was decorated in 2010, in recognition of her 40 years as Children's Society Secretary.

Below: The Bishop presides over a celebratory service during the 2005 patronal flower festival.

Chapter V

The Church and the Tudors

The year 1491 saw the birth of a King that was to change the face of religion in this country. After succeeding his father in 1509, Henry VIII became passionate about making himself the most powerful person in the land. A well-educated and intelligent man, Henry's pastimes included jousting, wrestling, dancing, gambling and hunting to name but a few. He was also a sportsman, author and composer. As his love of parties and banquets took its toll on him, in the later years of his reign, he became fat, bloated and riddled with disease. He eventually died in 1547.

Henry VIII married Catherine of Aragon and instantly wanted her to bear a son to carry on the House of Tudor. Their first born daughter was Mary and after still births and miscarriages, it became clear that Catherine was now too old to produce a son. Thus Henry requested a divorce but the Pope refused. This was the beginning of the turbulent ride that would see the Act of Supremacy formed in 1534. In short it made him *"the only supreme head on earth of the church in England"*. This meant that all ties with Rome and Roman Catholicism were cut, provoking huge unrest. The Protestant denomination of Christianity was used to form the new "Church of England", of which the King was head. It is said that Catherine was related to the Roman Emperor and therefore Pope Clement VII again refused the divorce and as a result Henry's desire for power was complemented by the new Treason Act which made it a crime to deprive the King of his wishes. 1544 finally saw Henry achieve complete power as he became known as "Defender of the Faith" a title still given to the monarch today.

The Act created huge tensions among faithful people the country over. But none more so than in 1536 in the North of England. The event which was to become known as the Pilgrimage of the Grace began on 13th of October of that year. It was led by Robert Aske who headed the 9,000 insurgents and marched on York where they took part in religious activity. In response, the Duke of Norfolk and Earl of Shrewsbury talked to the 40,000 assembled men. Aske trusted in the King's word, spoken through these two dignitaries, and dismissed his followers. Henry was not however true to his word and a new rising began. Aske was sentenced and killed, depriving the uprising of a leader. The King used his powers and his two aides to crush the revolt. However, worse was to come.

Henry died in 1547 and was briefly succeeded by his son Edward VI who was only nine years old when he came to the throne! After nine days of rule by Lady Jane Grey, Henry's first born daughter, Mary, came to the throne. Born in 1516 to first wife Catherine of Aragon she was a devout Catholic. She, like her family, was very intelligent, playing both the lute and spinet and speaking numerous languages. It is reported that she was very much like her father and had his cruel gene. She was a very unpopular Queen and even married Phillip of Spain: England's enemy.

She, again like her father, changed religion. The year after her coronation she repealed the Act of Supremacy and began converting subjects back to Roman Catholicism. Some sources claim that she hated the Church of England so much that she burned 300 Protestants to death[9].

1558 saw her death and her half-sister Elizabeth came to the throne. Elizabeth was Henry's daughter born to second wife Anne Bolyen in 1533. She inherited her father's intellect and was a wonderful writer, politician and even spoke five languages. Crowned Queen in 1558, she was only 25 years of age. Many people believed that she would be a weak leader because of her youth and gender but in actual fact she was tough and quick tempered. With reference to religion, she was a devout Protestant and before her death in 1603 ending the House of Tudor, she strengthened the Church of England. Upon her rise to the throne in 1558, she created a new Act of Supremacy and the Church of England has remained the main English religion ever since. "Supreme Governor of the Church of England" was her title.

In November of 1569, northern Catholic noblemen launched an attack on Elizabeth's crown, wishing to install Mary Queen of Scots as monarch; it was later to become known as the Rising of the North. In the North of England many of the gentry were Roman Catholic, meaning resentment of the new church and its head was strong, as demonstrated by the Pilgrimage of the Grace. The offensive was led by the Earls of Westmoreland and Northumberland, Charles Neville and Thomas Percy. They began by taking control of Durham Cathedral where they celebrated mass. Next, they moved south to Bramham Moor and on to the seizure of Barnard Castle.

Meanwhile, the Earl of Essex raised an army of 7,000 men who marched from York on December 13th. When combined with Baron Clinton's 12,000 men this resilience was enough to frighten the rebels; they dispersed with many fleeing to Scotland. In 1572 Thomas Percy was captured and then beheaded in York with Neville escaping and eventually dying in poverty. In excess of 600 supporters were killed by the Queen's order.

There were two executions in Fishburn, two in Bishop Middleham and five in Sedgefield but none recorded in Trimdon. The Reverend George Swalwell curate of St. Mary Magdalene was an open supporter of the rebels. He was condemned to death and was hung, drawn and quartered in Darlington, 29th July 1594.

During the reign of the House of Tudor, religion had changed completely. The Dissolution of the Monasteries in 1536 was to change it even further. Henry saw the monasteries as a sign of papal authority and had anxieties around this. In addition to this, they were the wealthiest institutions in the country owning approximately one third of the land in England and Wales. In 1535 Henry ordered Thomas Cromwell, the head of the church, to survey how much each of these institutions owned, known as Valor Ecclesiasticus.

In March 1536 a law was passed. It ordered that any monastery which included abbeys, priories, friaries and nunneries with an income of less than £200 per annum to be dissolved. Out of over 850 in operation 300 were closed. The remainder were required to give money to the King. Those that were closed were stripped of anything of value and the building fell into ruin. Any metals were taken and melted down with the other items being auctioned off. Within four years over 800 of the monasteries closed after intense pressure from the Government. Included in this was Guisborough Priory which owned St. Mary Magdalene. This resulted in a new chapter in church history.

Chapter VI

Farming, Vaults and Bells

Lord Humphrey Wharton was given the Parish of Trimdon in 1546, as a commendation of his bravery in the Scottish Wars. This was the first time anyone other than the Priory at Guisborough is recorded as owning the parish. It is unclear exactly when, but the Roper family bought the parish and built their family manor in Trimdon. The sale of the manor of Trimdon upon the death of Robert Roper in 1687 saw the estate pass to John Woodifield Esquire of Fishburn. In 1715 his daughter, Elizabeth, married William Beckwith of Thurcroft and the manor once again changed hands. Mr Beckwith became "of Trimdon" and his family have retained strong links ever since.

It was through the marriage of Mary Chalonder of Guisborough and another William Beckwith that William was born. He had three brothers – John, Edward and Matthew; alongside five sisters – Mary, Elizabeth, Susanna, Margaret and Dorothy. William married Elizabeth on 28th April 1715 and gained the manor. They had three children: William, Maria and Elizabeth. The family lived many years in Trimdon and even today the Patron of St. Mary Magdalene and indeed Trimdon Village is Rupert Beckwith Moore. One source states that the Beckwith family began the vault underneath the chancel floor in 1828. During renovations to St. Mary Magdalene in order to level the floor for a carpet to be laid, it was discovered in 1989.

It is inscribed on the flyleaf of the Trimdon Burial register, *"The entrance to Mr Beckwith's family vault is fifteen feet from the end of the chancel, in a straight line between the east window and the north-east corner."*[9] The excavations unearthed two concrete slabs marking the entrance. After some debate, as it is a resting place, the Reverend John Williamson allowed the opening of the vault. The vault is constructed of hand-made bricks and lying inside were five coffins – four adult-sized and one child's, packed with wood shavings. After photographs and short prayers, it was closed. The main points that make this discovery intriguing begin with the packing material. The coffins of the Beckwith family are packed in wood shavings which was, at the time, considered unusual. Secondly, the coffins appeared to have been disturbed. One coffin was placed on its side and another touching the bottom step. For more information on the Beckwith Family vault see appendix A.

There has been much debate over the years among villagers about tunnels under the church. Some believe that a tunnel was constructed between Tremeduna Grange (formerly a farm) and the church, to be used by the monks who lived there. It has even been said that there is a tunnel all the way to Durham Cathedral. At the time of the vault discovery none of these were found.

The 18th century saw farming continue in Trimdon before the looming Industrial Revolution would change the face of the village forever.

There is a brass plaque located in the chancel bearing a Latin inscription. It tells of the burial of Bryan Lancaster (Curate) and is the oldest fitting in the church, dated 1759. The current bell is also dedicated to his memory.

The children of St. Mary Magdalene Sunday School, 2000 years after Christ's birth in the year 2000.

John Burton (Churchwarden) and Prime Minister Tony Blair enjoy the flowers at the 2005 flower festival: "Fishers of Men".

Prime Minster Tony Blair alongside French Premier Lionel Jospin who served as French Prime Minster from 1997-2002 and visited the church in 1998.

Prospect Terrace, Trimdon. 4175

Prospect Terrace (now part of Front Street South) with St. Mary Magdalene's wall at the left.

Chapter VII

Smoke of the Black Diamond

Henry VIII had changed religion forever but the 19th century was one of both cultural and social transformation in Trimdon. It would also see huge change at St. Mary Magdalene, providing an average Norman church with unique and intriguing charisma. The century began with a county, and indeed country, entirely different to those at the end, presided over by the longest reigning monarch of all time: Queen Victoria.

County Durham, and indeed Trimdon, had rural economies focused around farming and wool. The county became a hotspot of manufacturing and mining. More and more collieries opened in the county, ushering in a new age of wealth and prosperity for the region. In 1843 the first coal was drawn from Five Houses, a hamlet to the north of the old village. Two years later Joseph Smith sank a mine on the same site. This village was to grow and become known as Trimdon Grange after the large house. A new industrial Trimdon was born and rapidly expanded. It did, however, bring its own problems such as housing. Houses were poorly and quickly constructed in the absence of building regulations. Running water was never seen and living conditions were poor. The Times newspaper's report of a cholera outbreak in 1854 is an example of how these conditions led to tragedy. A railway station opened at New Trimdon – another offspring of the old village – and the name Trimdon Station was coined. 1870 saw another mine sunk at Deaf Hill a few miles east of Trimdon Grange. This mining revolution swept across the coal-rich county. It was a very dangerous industry as witnessed on February 16th 1882 when an explosion killed over 70 men and boys at Trimdon Grange Colliery. This event was immortalised by the

Tommy Armstrong song – *The Trimdon Grange Explosion*. This came one year after a peak workforce of 700 was recorded.

The new industries of the county did not stop there, with engineering pioneers developing new technologies to improve the mining industry. 1825 saw the opening of the Darlington and Stockton Railway, the first passenger railway in the world, making the North East famous as the father of the railways. In Cleveland, iron ore was providing a booming industry and blast furnaces began to appear. Ship building increased on Tyneside and at its peak was providing two fifths of the world's tonnage.

The Durham Coalfield reached its peak in 1913 mining 41 million tonnes. This big boost in employment brought many people to the region from places such as Derbyshire, Wales, Ireland and Yorkshire to name but a few. 1,596 people lived in Trimdon in 1851 which increased to 3,266 in 20 years. This was also the case in the whole of County Durham from 161,035 in 1851 to 273,671 in 1871.

Although Trimdon Village did not have a colliery as a result of its geology, many of its peoples were employed in those of Trimdon Grange and Fishburn. A newly-renovated memorial to those killed in the Trimdon Grange Explosion was rededicated in the East Cemetery by the Bishop of Durham, the Right Reverend David Jenkins in 1991.

It was also a century of change for the church of St. Mary Magdalene. The century began with the renovation and redecoration in 1806 and the installation of pews. Despite this new breath of life, the historian Fordyce in his book: A History of Durham from 1855 recorded it as:

> *"The church which stands in the middle of the village,*
> *is a ruinous neglected looking edifice, consisting of a*
> *nave, chancel with bell turret at the west. There are two*

*modern arched, sash windows in the chancel and three
of similar construction on the south side of the building,
the north being completely blank. In the interior the
furniture is plain and common with texts of scripture
hung upon the walls. The church is exceedingly damp
and the only indications of recent attention to the edifice
are a coat of yellow ochre in the interior and an external
whitewashing."*

After that terrible report, the future of St. Mary Magdalene began to unfold. Mr Robert Borrowdale of Darlington was the chosen builder to complete the alteration works of 1873. The work commenced in July of that year with the construction of a north aisle. This section raised the seating capacity from 90 to 150, joined to the original nave by three pointed arches. The door into the chancel from the outside was installed. The vestry was added and remained in use until it was extended in 2010. The outside "rough cast" was removed, the stone repointed and an open drain constructed around the building. The floor was lifted and black and red Staffordshire tiles were inserted. The Leper window was glazed as a gift of Edward Hardy (Churchwarden). Next, at a cost of £15, the porch was demolished and reconstructed. The flat ceiling was removed and the current open-beamed roof was installed. Finally, the wooden window frames described by Fordyce were removed and replaced by the stone ones seen today, fitted with thick cathedral glass[11]. All of this building work really changed the character of the church from a boring Norman building to a lived-in and loved place of worship. To complete this amazing century, a new pulpit was dedicated. The original pulpit, made of stone, donated by Mr R. Forster, was removed making way for the new wooden design. The members of St. Cuthbert's Quilting Club installed the current pulpit as their gift in 1895. A century of change had been witnessed by the little church on the green in which the dove of the Holy Spirit had given new life to the "edifice"[12].

Chapter VIII

100 years of love

The one thousand and nine hundredth year since the birth of Christ began the 20th century: a time of technological advances, civil and human rights, freedom and of course war. It was also to be a century of challenge for the Church across the world. By the end of the century the world was a smaller place, with the advances in communication and transportation technology and globalisation. A century had begun which would witness war after war alongside freedom from dictatorship, communism and colonialism, scarred by breaches of human rights and acts of terrorism. Life at the beginning was almost unrecognisable, with numerous social changes taking place: women, minorities and homosexuals were beginning to find equality and class barriers were beginning to be removed.

St. Mary Magdalene continued to evolve throughout the century providing its mission to an ever-changing community. In 1913 the current mosaic reredos and altar were added. The chancel was further improved in 1919 with the installation of choir stalls. This resulted in the organ in the chancel being relocated to the right of the nave. It was originally installed in 1910, manufactured by the famous County Durham factory Harrison and Harrison. Later in 1960, Rodger Paul installed the current altar rails in memory of his wife Ethel. He also donated the eagle lectern which is not only a feature of St. Mary Magdalene but also St. Alban, Trimdon Grange and the former church of St. Paul, Trimdon Colliery.

Throughout the century, kind villagers who took pride in their church, donated fittings in memory of their loved ones including:

the votive candle stand, the hymn number boards and hymn book stand. One of the more noticeable is the Ruth Window. Located on the south side of the nave, this bright and colourful window was installed in 1929. It depicts Ruth and Naomi from the Bible. Ruth was the wife of an Israelite and upon his death showed deep devotion to the family and therefore God. Through her second marriage she became the great-grandmother of the famous Israelite King David. It is inscribed with the Bible quotation: *"Let me now go to the field and clean ears of corn after him in whose sight I will find grace."* Ruth 2:2. It was installed by local farmer and Churchwarden Robert Wearmouth Parker in memory of his beloved wife Margaret.

It was decided to replace the Harrison and Harrison with a modern light oak instrument in 1982. The new organ, installed at the back of the church, has an unusual juxtaposition of the black and white keys and was dedicated in October 1982 by the Bishop of Jarrow.

The 1980s also saw the relaying of the floor and, of course, the discovery of the Beckwith Family vault in 1989. The choir stalls were removed leaving the chancel free for meetings and functions. The floor was levelled and entirely carpeted.

The famous County Councillor George (Mick) Terrans was a Trimdon legend and went from miner to County Council leader. He has been remembered by family, friends and colleagues with the installation of a modern stained-glass window. It is located on the south side of the chancel next to the leper window.

The Second World War ended in 1945 and the names of those from Trimdon Village killed in action were immortalised on a brass plaque. It was originally located on the eastern wall of the north aisle. In 2010 when the north aisle extension and toilet were added the plaque moved to the adjacent wall, beneath the British Legion standards.

The century also saw change on the outside. The churchyard, once a coffin-shape built in the green had become overgrown and a disgrace – it is even reported that people used to dump their waste over its walls. The mature trees were felled and the vegetation removed. The old walls were taken away, with the exception of the south and west walls. The gravestones were removed in order for grass cutting to take place; they have been used to form a perimeter wall at the eastern edge. This new appearance which was greatly smarter afforded the church third place in the tidy churchyard competition and aided the village in its success in the tidy pit village awards. A huge transformation from the days of Fordyce.

To genuflect is to bend your knee. In church it has long been a tradition to kneel whilst praying. In St. Mary Magdalene long, thin kneelers hung from the pews: to make the process more comfortable. In the 1980s it was decided that the traditional kneelers were too thin and that they should be replaced. Hand-worked tapestry-style cushions were chosen. Parishioners bought the kits and began creating the wonderful array of designs we see today. Each handmade masterpiece was donated to the church in memory of a loved one and shows a dedication to them on the underneath. A large amount of interesting and colourful designs and patterns were made including: Easter, Remembrance and Christmas, to plain crosses, landscapes and shields. Special designs were commissioned for the altar rail, Churchwarden, and for use at weddings. They continue to be used today and tell an intriguing story to visitors and congregation members alike.

In the late 1960s the coal industry began to decline and collieries such as Trimdon Grange and Bowburn began to close. This loss of employment provided mass unemployment and huge social problems. Trimdon Grange fell into category D for investment, meaning no money was spent on its regeneration. It was removed from this category in 1970 and has since been redeveloped.

In 1983 a new parliamentary constituency was created for Sedgefield. Anthony Charles Lynton Blair was selected to represent the new constituency at the General Election for the Labour Party. In 1994, after the death of John Smith, Tony Blair was elected leader of the Labour Party. It was only three years until he led the party to victory in 1997 and became Prime Minister. In August of that year, Princess Diana of Wales was killed in a car crash in Paris. Tony Blair was attending St. Mary Magdalene Church the following morning. With the church as the backdrop he delivered his "People's Princess" speech. Over 24 years as Member of Parliament, he visited the church many times describing it in his memoirs as *"a beautiful church with one of the few surviving Norman arches around its altar, a pretty garden and graveyard."*[13] He constantly chose Trimdon to make speeches and this resulted in the village being put on the world map.

In the stonework that creates the church building, small holes can be observed. They are home to tiny bees. Their sting cannot penetrate human skin and they are known as masonry bees. The church provides the ideal conditions for them to live with its sandstone rubble walls. It is thought to be the female who makes her nest in the masonry, making little holes in the stonework. She then uses it to breed and new bees emerge.

The annual gift day collection at the village shops.

The path from the west end of the churchyard across the green (no longer there).

Above: Parishioners take part in a sponsored walk in aid of the Children's Society in 2010.

Left: St. Mary Magdalene as depicted in the stained glass window of 1873.

©D. Spears

Chapter IX

The 21st Century and still proud

Trimdon has come a long way in the last 850 years since the church was constructed. Villagers posed with Prime Minister Tony Blair to celebrate the millennium, 2,000 years since the birth of Christ. The then Prime Minister donated a bench outside Tremeduna Grange in celebration of 100 years of a working class voice through the Labour Party. Here people can sit on the spot where the ancient monks lived and Italian prisoners of war were held during the Second World War. Their view is of St. Mary Magdalene Church standing proud, the queen of the village, on her island, raised above the sweeping village green. From the outside, a desirable place for ceremonies and from the inside, a place of worship, of faith and a place of historical importance to the culture of Trimdon Village and the local community.

Accessibility has been a recurring issue throughout the first decade; each improvement making it easier to use the building. The refreshment centre makes it easier for functions to be held in church. The uneven pavement was removed from the outside of the church door and new level paving laid, meaning wheelchairs and pushchairs can enter the building with ease. A new interior glass door floods the church with natural light and was the kind gift of Mrs Peggy Robinson MBE in memory of her husband and local historian W. Robinson.

After the completion of this project it was felt by the church council that an accessible toilet was needed. In 2007 the "Loo and Vestry Appeal" was launched to raise £75,000. The community came together and expressed their pride for their church. The money was raised through many kind donations from local businesses and families along with local and national grants. The work was completed in November 2010. An American white oak door was installed in the north aisle, donated by former Churchwarden W. Anderson and his wife Licensed Pastoral Assistant E. Anderson. The new facilities have been twinned with a toilet in Burundi. The scheme "Bogs for Burundi" has meant that parishioners can make a real difference to the thousands of people who do not have the safe and sanitary conditions that we take for granted. The vestry was extended to the east enlarging the usable space. This has provided a new home for Sunday School and other groups in the future.

The 25th Patronal Flower Festival was themed around "Celebration" in 2008. After 25 wonderful years, it was decided to end the festival. The Patronal Festival continues to be marked with a programme of special events, on the closest weekend to July 22nd.

The biggest change in the 21st century has been the formation of the Upper Skerne Parish. In the 1990s the three Trimdon churches of St. Paul, St. Alban and St. Mary Magdalene became Trimdon Benefice. So, St. Mary Magdalene went from Parish church under the control of Reverend John Williamson to part of the new benefice under the Reverend Peter Baldwin. Canon Alex Whitehead was also vicar of the combined parish from 1999 to 2003. The Church of England has a decreasing number of clergy due to falling funds. At the time of Canon Whitehead's departure the diocese was promoting the increase in pastoral assistants, lay readers and part-time clergy. The Parishes of Sedgefield, Fishburn and Bishop Middleham joined with the Trimdon Benefice to form a locality. Then on 19th April, 2005 the locality officially merged to form The Parish of The Upper Skerne by a pastoral measure. This brought St. Alban, Trimdon Grange, St. Paul, Trimdon Colliery, St. Mary Magdalene, Trimdon Village, St. Catherine, Fishburn, St. Edmund, Sedgefield and St.

Michael and All Angels, Bishop Middleham together as one combined parish under a single ministry team.

The ministry team is comprised of the Rector, Reverend Michael Gobett, a team vicar and sometimes a curate. This clergy team is supported by lay readers. The Reverend Adrian Thorpe was the first team vicar and was succeeded by Reverend Phillip Tait. Other clergy have included curates Reverend John Williamson and Reverend Alison Richardson along with non-stipendiary clergy in Reverend Helen Thorpe and Reverend John Rogers.

The new parish has brought a new dimension to worship. New services such as Communion by Extension, Services of the Word and Baptisms within the communion services are but a few. Sadly, since the formation of the new parish, St. Paul's has closed, despite every effort to save it. The building is as yet unsold.

Despite a rise in average Sunday attendance in the first decade of the new century, 2009 saw the first ever deficit on its balance sheet – a trend that is set to escalate in the future. This church, which is the pride of the village, needs tremendous continuing support; but I know that the kind, decent and thoughtful people of Trimdon, who are current stewards of this once "neglected-looking edifice"[14], will want to ensure that another 850 years of history can be recorded!

The original, coffin-shaped, churchyard was much larger than the modern one.

The old village: with the church as its centrepiece.

An historical re-enactment takes place on the village green.

The old village, simply one street with the church at the centre.

*The annual flower festival was a much-loved village event
for 25 years.*

Postscript by Tony Blair

It was, during my 24 years as Sedgefield MP, my absolute pleasure to experience the delights of St. Mary Magdalene Church – the Eucharist, the Flower Festivals and the Good Friday Passion Procession to St. Williams RC Church, to mention but a few.

The French Prime Minister, Lionel Jospin, called in during his visit to the constituency and really appreciated the building. He said that on his return to France he would try and find another example of a "Norman Horseshoe Arch" similar to the one in the chancel. And, of course, it was on that fateful morning of Diana's death that I delivered the "People's Princess" speech to the world's media, from the green outside the church.

I am touched to be part of the history of such a fine building, and feel sure that the determination and kindness of the people of Trimdon will ensure its future survival.

850 years have witnessed some immense changes, and I wish everyone connected with St. Mary Magdalene's good luck for many more years of church life.

Appendix A

The Beckwith Family Vault

Adapted from a Short Account by Rev. John Williamson (1989)

Several people had told me about a tunnel – or tunnels – under the chancel floor in St. Mary Magdalene Church at Trimdon. They were said to go to the Fox & Hounds and secondly to Tremeduna Grange, the site of the farm where the monks from Guisborough used to live and lastly to Durham Cathedral. If they all really existed, the church would have more tunnelling than British Coal – and the diocese would probably long ago have sunk down in subsidence! The story about one to the old farm was more credible. After all, those old monks said their services at very strange hours – and they might have wanted a covered way into church.

Then, while searching through old records at County Hall, I discovered some entries handwritten in the front of an old burials register, (Burial Register commencing 7th February 1813): *"The entrance to Mr Beckwiths' Family Vault is fifteen feet from the end of the chancel, in a straight line between the east window and north east Corner"*. *"Finished February 6th, 1828" "RD"*. I worked out *"RD"* must be Roddam Douglas who, it appears, was a vicar of this parish, or as they were called at that time, the Curate of this parish.

Whether or not there was a tunnel under the church floor, there certainly was a vault somewhere! The trouble was that "fifteen feet from the end of the chancel" could mean that it was in the chancel itself – or out in the nave, under the pews. And did "north east corner" mean of the church or of the chancel? And how big a vault would it be?

The chancel floor had been very uneven for some years and was gradually getting worse. It was now difficult, if not dangerous, to

Excavations begin as the tiles are removed.

A crack began to appear at the edge of the slabstone.

walk on. The church architect had therefore said it should be levelled and given specifications, about depth of excavation, materials to be used, etc. We were about to put into church a new carpet costing thousands of pounds, so the floor had to be levelled first. We expected that work to cost many hundreds of pounds – probably a thousand. Then, lo and behold!, two village men, Jackie Dunn and Phil Robinson (Trimdon Floor Screeders), volunteered to do the job free of all labour costs! Their generous offer was accepted eagerly. Work in church has to have approval from the Diocesan authorities and from the Chancellor of the Diocese – a kind of ecclesiastical judge. We worked our way through all the rules and regulations and formal approvals, and the time came to start on the work itself – under supervision from both the church architect and an archaeologist. Dennis Coggins, who retired from Bowes Museum in November 1988 agreed to act as archaeological consultant for us. He charged us nothing either!

The day before excavation of the floor started, Easter Monday 1989, there was no sign of what was to come. Under the narrow strip of carpet leading through the chancel there was an old stone with some indecipherable writing on it. That looked a hopeful place for discoveries. Jackie and Phil began to remove the tiles as carefully as they could, in the hope that they could be replaced on the new floor. Unfortunately, this turned out to be impossible because of the way they had been originally laid – set straight on to concrete, which itself had been roughly laid on a load of rubble and old building material. Everyone was eager to lift the old stone in the middle, but we had to wait until Dennis Coggins arrived. Soon he came, the stone was lifted – and nothing at all was found!

After the tiles were cleared, the rubble underneath had to be tackled. As the work progressed on Tuesday, two concrete slabs were uncovered, together with some signs of an original cobbled/slabbed floor. This floor was on the same level as the nave floor is now. The

The crack became larger.

Signs of an earlier low-level floor were discovered.

stonework around the entrance to the vestry didn't reach down to that level, showing that the vestry was built after the floor level was raised, probably at the same time as the north aisle was built. The slabstones sounded hollow and lifting them was discussed, but the archaeologist asked that the whole floor be cleared to the same level before they were touched, so that a proper full picture could be got. This work continued on Wednesday. A cavity soon began to appear at the edge of the slabs!

Now, the final decision on raising them had to be made. That wasn't as straightforward as people might think. Raising them might lead on to more excavation – and we needed the church for Sunday services! In the end I decided that we should go ahead as no one else is likely to see that level of floor for many years – if at all – though I stipulated that no further excavation could take place.

No more excavation was necessary! We found steps leading down from near the north side altar rail into what looked just like a tunnel. Without a light, the back wall of the vault could not be seen. The first thoughts were that we had found "the tunnel". But it wasn't, even though it was tunnel-shaped, made from a mixture of stone and hand-made bricks which had been roughly plastered together. Inside were five coffins, four of adults and one of a child.

The archaeologist began to take measurements and photographs, as did Peggy Robinson and I all under the watchful eye of the Churchwarden Emeritus, Fred Slater, who had attended the church for a lifetime of 80-plus years without knowing about the vault. No one living did, though some had talked of seeing a "tunnel" once. The only noteworthy thing about the coffins was that the bodies had been packed in wood shavings. The archaeologist had not come across that before. The coffins themselves were breaking up and disintegrating to a large extent. We therefore left them alone. One coffin was packed in on its side and another was partly resting on the bottom step. That one had been covered in some kind of cloth material which was now just mould. It also had a very badly corroded coat of arms on it; but it was so corroded that nothing of it could be made out.

I was very conscious that this place was a burial ground and, interesting as it undoubtedly was, it was not the place for sightseeing or curiosity. So, as soon as the archaeologist had finished, a record of our visit was left behind in the vault (double sealed in two polythene bags), a short re-committal service was taken, the stones were replaced and the vault was resealed. Many people I know were disappointed not to have seen it, but it is after all the last resting place of five people.

The old stone can still be seen in the floor under the carpet. When the light shines on it in a certain way, it seems to have the name "Donnison" on it, we think. There is an entry in the burials register which says: *"Elizabeth Donnison, late Sparke, of Trimdon in ye Family Vault in the Church here. Wife of Watson Stote Donnison, Clerk, aged 50 years. Died 22nd March 1798 and buried 27th March 1798"* There is also an entry which says: *"Elizabeth Margaret Rowe, 2nd Daughter of Thomas Rowe and Maria Jemima Donnison. Interred in the Family Vault within the Parish Church of Trimdon. Died 9th August 1812 and buried on 14th August 1812, aged 2½ years"* Other members of that family are recorded in the registers: "Sparke Hughes from the Parish of Sunderland, 3rd daughter of the Revd. Watson Stote Donnison, late of this parish and wife of Johnson [indecipherable] Hughes, Mariner. Died 15th March 1807 and buried 18th March 1807, aged 31 years" – and – "James Donnison Hughes, son of Johnson and Sparke Hughes; died 15th June 1807, buried 18th June 1807, aged 1½ years". There are others too – eight in all from the Donnison family. And there is the entry which goes with my first clue about the vault: *"Julie Beckwith of Trimdon House, Parish of Sedgefield, buried 6th February 1828*

The steps from the north side altar rail lead down into the vault.

Five coffins of Beckwith family members were discovered.

Above: A coat of arms can be seen on the coffin. Sadly it was too corroded to read.

Left: The kind members of Trimdon Floor Screeders pause for a photograph after discovering the vault.

aged 18". She fits in with the Revd. Roddam Douglas's entry stating that the Beckwith Family vault was completed in 1828.

So some questions remain unanswered. What is the connection between the Beckwiths and the Donnisons – if any? Or are there two family vaults under the church? Just who is buried in the vault we have found? And what about the old Vicar, Bryan Lancaster? He is buried there somewhere too.(Seen on the brass plate on the south wall of the chancel). The burials register records him: **"Bryan Lancaster, Curate, buried 11th November, 1759"**.

Who knows?: there may still be a tunnel after all...

The Rev. John Williamson conducts a service of re-committal.

Timeline of the history
of the Church of Mary Magdalene, Trimdon

43AD	Christianity comes to Britain with the Romans
994AD	King Canute born
995AD	Durham Diocese formed
1093	First block laid at Durham Cathedral
C1145	Current building started
1534	First Act of Supremacy
1536	Pilgrimage of the Grace
1546	Trimdon Manor awarded to Lord Humphrey Wharton
1558	Second Act of Supremacy passed
1594	Rev. George Swalwell hung, drawn and quartered
1687	Trimdon Manor passes to John Woodifield
1715	The Beckwith family become "of Trimdon" and take control of the manor.
1758	Parsonage built
1759	Bryan Lancaster (Curate) dies
1806	Church renovated and pews added
1828	Beckwith Vault said to have been constructed

1873	North aisle added and other works (see chapter VII)
C1880	New stone font installed
1895	The current pulpit donated by St. Cuthbert's Quilting Club
1910	Harrison Harrison organ installed
1913	Current altar installed
1919	Choir stalls added to the chancel
1929	Ruth Window donated by R. Wearmouth Parker
1960	Altar rail and lectern dedicated
1982	Organ replaced and dedicated by the Bishop
1989	The church was completely carpeted and during the floor levelling the Beckwith Family vault was discovered
1997	Princess Diana is killed. Prime Minister Tony Blair uses the church as the backdrop for his speech
1998	French Prime Minister, Lionel Jospin visits church on his visit to the constituency.
2000	The millennium was celebrated with a photo shoot on the village green
2005	The Parish of the Upper Skerne was formed and St. Mary Magdalene joined the other 5 churches as one parish
2006	A new internal door, refreshment centre and portable font were installed
2010	An accessible toilet installed and the vestry extended at a cost of £75,000

Appendix C

Incumbents of the Trimdon Parish

C1501	John Senhouse
C1570-76	John Buckle
1576-78	George Swalwell
1578	Ra Anterburne
1579	George Morden
1587	John Martin
1613	William Fisher
1632	William Lister
1641	William Fisher
1673-95	Stephen Woodifield
1695-1709	Robert Adamson
1709-52	William Woodifield
1752-59	Bryan Lancaster
1759-63	William Dunn
1763-83	Benjamin Darwin
1783	Edward Davison
1789-97	William Gilfrid Gates
1806-16	John Ebdon
1818-20	Adam Harry
1821-40	Roddam Douglas
1840-46	William Norval
1846-75	George Sproston
1869-71	L Broughton (Curate)
1871	Oates Sagar
1875	RN Simpson
1879	George Lloyd
1876-91	E Coltier Biggs
1891-1905	James Marmaduke Hick
1905	R H Smallwood
1905-17	William Jackson Whitehead

1917-24	Fredrick Albert Rainbow
1924-35	A Davison
1935-53	Ernest Folio Montague Baker
1953-55	Henry Fox Riley
1956-60	Herbert Walker Langford
1960-69	Canon Stanley Landreth
1969-74	Ronald Sargison
1975-79	Nigel Tindale
1979-87	James David Hargreves
1988-94	John Williamson

Benefice of the Trimdons

| 1997-98 | Peter Baldwin |
| 1999-2003 | Canon Alex Whitehead |

From 2005 the clergy of the newly-formed Upper Skerne Parish have been joined by lay readers and non-stipendiary clergy to form a Ministry team, which has served St. Mary Magdalene.

The Reverend Peter Baldwin, first vicar of the Trimdon Benefice.

©An extract taken from "A brief history of St. Mary Magdalene, Trimdon" reproduced with kind permission of the chairman of Trimdon DCC.

Appendix D

An extract taken from *Thornyhold* by Mary Stewart.

"Until I was seven years old I had lived in a small village of two hundred souls or thereabouts. It was an unimportant little parish, and we were very poor, but the place was lovely, my father's work was easy, and the house was compact and comfortable. The vicarage that was ancient, low and white, with a white rose rambling over the porch… The Parish consisted mainly of farmland, farms scattered through a few square miles, with only one main road through it. Cars were rare; one walked, or went by pony trap. There were no buses, and the railway station was two miles away…

…The village green with its grazing goats and donkeys, and the **grey church in the centre**. Huge trees everywhere, on the green"

Stewart was born in 1916, daughter of the Reverend and Mrs Rainbow in Sunderland. One year later the Reverend took over the incumbency of Trimdon and Mary spent the next seven years in Trimdon. Thornyhold begins with a memory of Trimdon as seen above. Millions of her books have been sold across the world. Some 60 years after leaving Trimdon she was sent some photographs of the church. She responded in a letter to the then vicar: *"The Church! What a labour of love you have expanded there. It looks wonderful, shining and immaculate. I am so happy to see it, and know my dear father would have loved what you have done"*

References

1. Local legends discovered during research very little, weak evidence available.

2. A local legend however it is recorded in Roberts Johnson E., More Trimdon Snippets, 2000 page 6 and Durham County Council, Memories of Trimdon Village.

3. William Beveridge housing see www.psi.org.uk (Personal Studies Institute, University of Westminster).

4. Local Legend, weak evidence.

5. Bethany Christian Centre see www.bethanychristiancentre.co.uk

6. Emmanuel Church see www.emmanuel.org.uk.

7. Local legend but record in Trimdon DCC, A brief history of St Mary Magdalene Church, 2009 page 10.

8. See Durham County Advertiser February 6th 1874.

9. Weak printed evidence but see www.localhistories.org/tudor.

10. Taken from Trimdon Burial Register commencing 7th. February 1813 and ending 6th February 1828.

11. See Durham County Advertiser February 6th 1874.

12. Taken from Fordyce, A History of Durham, 1855.

13. Taken from Blair T., A Journey, 2010 page 139.

14. Taken from Fordyce W., A History of Durham, 1855.

Bibliography

BLAIR T., A Journey, Hutchinsons, 2010

Durham County Council, Heritage and History of County Durham, 1997

Trimdon DCC, A Brief History of St. Mary Magdalene, 2009

Durham County Council, The Durham Book, 1982

ROBERTS JOHNSON E., More Trimdon Snippets, Printability Publishing, 2000

PEVSNER N, The Buildings of England: County Durham revised by E. Williamson, Yale University Press, 1985

ROBINSON T., Kings and Queens, Red Fox, 2001

PHILLIPS C., Kings and Queens of Britain, Hermes House, 2009

PARRAGON, British History Encyclopaedia, 1999

ROBERTS JOHNSON E., Trimdon Snippets, Printability Publishing, 1998

ROBERTS JOHNSON E., Last of Trimdon Snippets, Printability Publishing, 2002

DK CHILDREN, Eyewitness Rocks and Minerals, 2000

ROBBERTS M., Who's been nibbling at our church?, 2009

DURHAM COUNTY COUNCIL, Memories of Trimdon Village WILLIAMSON J., A short account of the Beckwith Family Vault, 1989

DUNLOP D. AND NIXON P., Exploring Durham History, Breedon Books, 1998

RYDER P.F., Church of Mary Magdalene Trimdon – An Architectural Assessment, 1993

HELICON PUBLISHING, Hutchinson's Encyclopaedia 1998, 1997

BARTLEY P., Life in the Industrial Revolution, Hodder and Stoughton, 1987

GRUNDY J., Northern Pride, Granada Media, 2003

GUINNESS PUBLISHING, Guinness Book of the 20th Century, 1997

LACEY R., The Life and Times of Henry VIII, George Weidenfeld and Nicolson Ltd., 1972

FORDYCE W., A History of Durham, 1855

Jarold Publishing, Durham Cathedral, 2005

WHELLAN & Co., History and Topography of Durham, 1894

RYDER P.F., An architectural Watching Brief Summer 2010, 2010

COGGINS D., Trimdon Village Church, 1989

RAINBOW F.A., Trimdon Parochial Magazine, 1924

STEWART M., Thornyhold, Mackays of Chatham, 1988

Durham County Advertiser, Friday February 6th 1874

Kelly's Diary 1910

The Times 27th July 1854

Trimdon Baptism Register 1869-1959

Durham Parish Boundaries Map circa 1800

Trimdon Electoral Register 1833

Trimdon Limestone Quarry, 1992

Geographical Conservation Reviewzx

RYDER P.F., Phased Sketch Plan based on map provided by C. Downes

www.tudorhistory.org; www.historylearningsite.co.uk; www.ritchies.net; www.bbc.co.uk; www.naturalengland.org.uk; www.nationalarchives.gov.uk; www.durham.anglican.org; www.escombsaxonchurch.com; www.englandsnortheast.co.uk; www.keytothepast.info; www.trimdon.com; www.newadvent.org; www.psi.org; www.localhistories.org/tudor.

Messages of Supprt

❝❝Adam Luke has shown outstanding skills and personal qualities from his earliest primary school days. He possesses great resourcefulness, a passion for history and a love for his home community. It has always been his ambition to author a book and his talented skills as a writer have come together in this publication. How marvellous to see such effort from someone so young. It is clear that he has certainly been as busy as a bee and his praiseworthy dedication has allowed him to soar to such great heights. ❞❞

Mr D.R. Craig Headteacher Trimdon Junior School

❝❝Adam Luke is a young man who shows great passion for Trimdon Village and St Mary Magdalene Church. Adam's book is a great introduction to the history of the local community and is proof of the fact that Adam is not only a passionate young man but also a young man with a bright future ahead of him. Read *'Doves, Pigeons and Masonry Bees'* and be enthralled. ❞❞

Phil Wilson M.P. for Sedgefield

❝❝Adam Luke is the kind of person you automatically turn to if you want to get something done! He is a superb community activist and one glance at a list of his achievements makes you realise what a marvellous ambassador and fundraiser he is for Trimdon and the wider community. Adam has been particularly successful in raising funds for his Parish Church, St Mary Magdalene and his latest venture – this history of the church and village is yet another example of his creativity and entrepreneurship. ❞❞

Cllr. P. Brookes County Councillor

❝I am so thrilled to have had the privilege of supporting such a dedicated and tenacious young man, Adam Luke. To have achieved such heights is staggering and the process was so well executed and developed a tremendous amount of community spirit and ownership. Trimdon certainly does have a star in its midst! **❞**

Nickie Gott N.E. Entrepreneur of the Year (2009)

❝Adam is a true example of a social entrepreneur – someone who puts into action a great idea which is of benefit to the wider community. I applaud him and look forward to hearing about his future endeavours. **❞**

Dinah Bennett OBE Director International Centre for Entrepreneurship